6.08

planet EARTH

Earth's Natural Resources

By Amy Bauman

Science curriculum consultant: Suzy Gazlay, M.A.,
science curriculum resource teacher

Gareth Stevens
Publishing

Please visit our web site at www.garethstevens.com.
For a free catalog describing our list of high-quality books, call 1-800-542-2595 (USA)
or 1-800-387-3178 (Canada). Our fax: 1-877-542-2596

Library of Congress Cataloging-in-Publication Data available upon request from the publisher.

ISBN-13: 978-0-8368-8917-8 (lib. bdg.)
ISBN-10: 0-8368-8917-7 (lib. bdg.)
ISBN-13: 978-0-8368-8924-6 (softcover)
ISBN-10: 0-8368-8924-X (softcover)

This North American edition first published in 2008 by
Gareth Stevens Publishing
A Weekly Reader® Company
1 Reader's Digest Road
Pleasantville, NY 10570-7000 USA

This U.S. edition copyright © 2008 by Gareth Stevens, Inc. Original edition copyright © 2007 by ticktock Media Ltd.
First published in Great Britain in 2007 by ticktock Media Ltd., Unit 2, Orchard Business Centre, North Farm Road,
Tunbridge Wells, Kent, TN2 3XF United Kingdom

ticktock Project Editor: Ruth Owen
ticktock Picture Researcher: Ruth Owen
ticktock Project Designer: Elaine Wilkinson
With thanks to: Suzy Gazlay, Mark Sachner, and Elizabeth Wiggans

Gareth Stevens Editor: Jayne Keedle
Gareth Stevens Creative Director: Lisa Donovan
Gareth Stevens Graphic Designer: Alex Davis

Photo credits (t = top; b = bottom; c = center; l = left; r = right):
Ambient Images, Inc./Alamy: cover. Corbis: 13tr, 16-17 main. Drakewell Museum, Pennsylvania Historical & Museum
Commission: 10bl. FLPA: 7cr, 19c, 23br, 24tl, 24cl, 28bl. NaturePL: 24bl. NASA: 7br. Photodisc (Corbis): 9tl, 9tr.
Shutterstock: 1,3, 4l, 4tc, 4cc, 4bc, 4-5 main, 5tr, 5cr, 7tc, 7bl, 8br, 9clt, 9crt, 9crb,10-11 main, 12l, 13b, 15tr, 16cl, 16b,
17r all, 17b all, 19tr, 19cr, 19br, 21cb, 21tr, 21br, 22t, 24-25 main, 25tr, 25br, 26cl, 27c, 27bl, 28-29 main, 28tl, 29tl, 30-
31 all. Superstock: 6, 8t, 9clb, 10l, 14-15 main, 15br, 18-19 main, 20, 21ct, 22b, 26. ticktock Media Ltd: 4cb, 9cr, 11ct,
11tr, 11cr, 11br, 12ct, 23 map, 27cr, 29r. Wikipedia: 7tr.

Every effort has been made to trace copyright holders, and we apologize in advance for any omissions. We would be pleased
to insert the appropriate acknowledgments in any subsequent edition of this publication.

Printed in the United States of America

1 2 3 4 5 6 7 8 9 10 09 08 07

CONTENTS

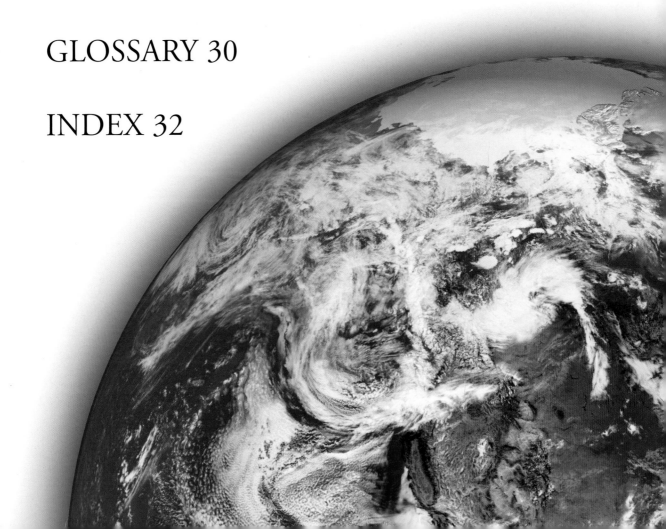

CHAPTER 1:
Our Planet's Bounty

Look around you. Everything in your daily life can be traced back to Earth's natural resources. Natural resources are the materials and sources of energy that come from our planet. Your toothbrush, the food you eat, the clothes you wear, the heat in your home—they all come from Earth's natural resources.

GIFTS THAT KEEP ON GIVING

As their name tells us, Earth's resources all come from nature. They include water, plant and animal life, coal, oil, **minerals**, and energy from wind and the Sun.

FRUIT
Fruit, like all plant resources, draws energy from the Sun.

FISH
Fish are among the many resources found in Earth's seas.

WATER
People, animals, and plants need water to survive.

WIND POWER
Like water and the Sun, wind is a renewable resource and can be used to generate electricity.

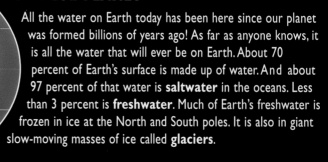

THE BLUE PLANET

All the water on Earth today has been here since our planet was formed billions of years ago! As far as anyone knows, it is all the water that will ever be on Earth. About 70 percent of Earth's surface is made up of water. And about 97 percent of that water is **saltwater** in the oceans. Less than 3 percent is **freshwater**. Much of Earth's freshwater is frozen in ice at the North and South poles. It is also in giant slow-moving masses of ice called **glaciers**.

People need Earth's natural resources to survive. We also depend on them to provide everything that helps make our lives more comfortable and enjoyable. We need to take care of these resources. We must make sure that they will continue to be available in the future.

Even a small area of land contains many natural resources. What resources do you see in this photo?

A WEALTH OF RESOURCES

SOIL
Farmers value rich soil as an important resource. Crops need good soil to grow. Farmers work to keep soil healthy and to protect it from **erosion** (wearing away).

DIAMONDS
Diamonds are among the minerals called **gemstones**. Like other minerals, they occur naturally. People value diamonds and other gems because they are so beautiful and difficult to find.

ALMOST ANYTHING IMAGINABLE
Everything these moviegoers are enjoying comes from natural resources. The fabric and metal in the seats come from plants and minerals. The popcorn comes from fields of corn. Even the film in the projector is made from **petroleum**!

DEFINING NATURAL RESOURCES

Natural resources may be grouped in several ways. One way is to list them as either **renewable** or **nonrenewable resources**. Renewable resources are those that nature can replace, recycle, or regrow in a short time. Animals, plants, water, and energy from the Sun and wind are examples of renewable resources. Remember, though, that even renewable resources can be used up if we waste them.

Fish from oceans, rivers, and lakes are a renewable resource. However, overfishing is threatening the survival of some fish, such as the tuna shown here.

Most trees are a renewable resource. Some trees, however, take a long time to grow. This old redwood has been growing for hundreds of years. Old-growth trees are considered to be nonrenewable.

Nature needs millions of years to create nonrenewable resources. They include oil, coal, natural gas, gold, silver, and other minerals. Today, people are using up these resources more quickly than nature can replace them. When our supply of nonrenewable resources runs out, there won't be more.

SOIL—WHAT KIND OF RESOURCE IS IT?

Some natural resources are not easy to list as either renewable or nonrenewable. Soil is one example. Although many people consider soil nonrenewable, it can be renewed. But it takes many years. Nature may need thousands of years to make 1 inch (2.5 cm) of healthy, mineral-rich soil.

THE QUAGGA: EXTINCT

Thousands of zebra-like animals called quagga once grazed on the plains of southern Africa. They were hunted in such large numbers that by 1870, none remained. They had become **extinct**.

HAWAIIAN BIRDS THREATENED

The mongoose was brought to Hawaii in 1883 to help control the islands' rat population. Mongooses, however, prefer to eat birds' eggs. That threatens Hawaii's ground-nesting birds.

THE ARAL SEA: THREATENED

The Aral Sea sits on the border between Kazakhstan and Uzbekistan in central Asia. Over the last 30 years, this sea has lost more than half of its water volume. Since the 1960s, its water sources have been used for **irrigation**. These satellite images show the sea in August 1989 (left) and August 2003.

*Minerals are inorganic resources. An **ore** is a mineral that contains a valuable material, such as iron. Here, iron ore is heated to create steel in a process called smelting.*

ORGANIC RESOURCES

Natural resources can be grouped in another way—as either **organic** or **inorganic**. Organic resources come from **organisms**, or living things. These include plants and animals. Think about all of the ways to use organic resources in a day. You might wear clothes made out of cotton or lamb's wool. Lunch might be an apple and a cheese sandwich. You write your reports on paper, maybe at a desk—both of which are made out of wood.

SKYSCRAPING RESOURCES

The Sears Tower in Chicago, Illinois, is North America's tallest building. It stands 1,450 feet (442 meters) and 110 stories tall. It was built with 96,000 tons (68,946 metric tons) of steel. Steel is made from iron ore, an inorganic natural resource.

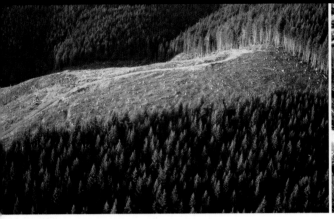

INORGANIC RESOURCES

Other natural resources are inorganic. Inorganic resources do not come from living organisms. Minerals and rocks are examples of inorganic materials. Our daily lives are filled with examples of these resources. The soda can you recycled today is made from aluminum. Construction crews use steel in buildings.

As a renewable organic resource, trees are often grown to be harvested. Whole forests may be grown (left) to be cut down for wood. The planting of new crops of trees (right) makes sure that these valuable resources stay renewable.

WOOL—AN ORGANIC RESOURCE
Wool is only one product that comes from sheep. We also eat their meat and make cheese and yogurt from their milk.

Sheep grow a fleece.

The sheep is sheared.

The fleece is spun into wool.

Wool is made into clothes and other textiles.

ORGANIC OR INORGANIC?

ⓘ In simple terms, *organic* means anything that comes from a plant or an animal. *Inorganic* describes anything that was never living.

Examine the following list and decide whether each item listed comes from an organic or inorganic resource.

1 drinking glass
2 honey
3 icicle
4 cooking oil made from corn or sunflowers

5 leather ball
6 mobile phone
7 spaghetti sauce
8 silk

What other items can you add to this list to stump your friends?

ANSWERS: 1. inorganic 2. organic 3. inorganic 4. organic 5. organic 6. inorganic 7. organic 8. organic

Natural gas forms along with oil. Today, people know natural gas is a useful natural resource. Early oil drillers, though, considered it worthless. They burned it just to get rid of it!

CHAPTER 2:
Nonrenewable Resources

Nonrenewable resources cannot be replaced easily or quickly. They are found on Earth in limited amounts. Even so, people have been using some of them at an increasing rate for years.

FOSSIL FUELS

Fossil fuels are nonrenewable resources. They include oil, natural gas, and coal. They are called fossil fuels because they began as the decaying remains of animals, plants, and other organisms.

Some of that organic matter fell to the ocean floor. It was covered over by **sediment**, or small bits of soil and sand. Some of the matter was buried deep in the ground. In either case, the decay was covered over by layer after layer of other materials. It all became part of Earth's **crust**, the hard outer layer of the planet's surface. There it sat for millions of years, compressed beneath the heat and weight of the matter covering it. Slowly the material formed fossil fuels.

DRILLING FOR OIL

The first oil well was drilled in Titusville, Pennsylvania, in 1859. There, a retired railroad conductor named Edwin Drake struck oil on his farm. At first, people were interested in oil for use in kerosene lamps. Use in cars and heating came later. Still, the modern oil industry began with Drake's discovery. His well was the first drilled just for the purpose of finding oil.

These rigs (below) drill for oil around the clock. We use oil in our cars and to heat our homes. The oil was formed from organisms that lived in water millions of years ago. Oil deposits found today might once have been covered by oceans or seas.

FOSSIL FUELS: WORLD CONSUMPTION 1965–2005

As this chart shows, the consumption of all fossil fuels (coal, gas, and oil) doubled between the 1960s and 2005. The rise of oil as a source of energy was less dramatic, especially compared to coal and natural gas. Note the use of two renewable resources: **hydroelectric power** (electricity generated by water power) and **nuclear energy** (energy released from atoms).

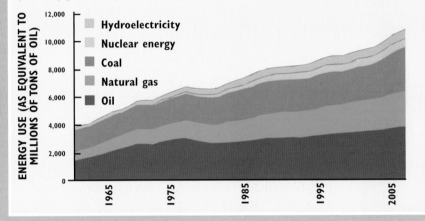

HOW COAL IS FORMED

SWAMP

PLANT DEBRIS

About 300 million years ago, tree-filled swamps covered much of Earth. As plants and trees died, they settled to the bottom of swamps. There, the matter began to decay.

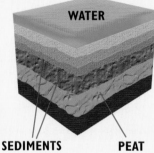

WATER

SEDIMENTS **PEAT**

The decaying matter formed peat. That spongy material was soon buried under more layers.

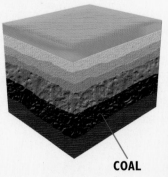

COAL

After millions of years of pressure and heat, the peat became coal.

USING FOSSIL FUELS

Roughly 80 percent of the energy used worldwide comes from fossil fuels. Most of these fossil fuels, such as oil, natural gas, and coal, must be changed in some way to create energy that we can use. Today, through technology, we are able to change fossil fuels to usable energy more efficiently.

Oil and natural gas are much in demand as energy sources. These fuels power our vehicles. They heat our homes and businesses. We also use these resources to make medicines, plastics, cosmetics, man-made fabrics, and other products.

You might be surprised by how many products are made with oil. It is used to make ink for printing money, asphalt for roads, lipstick, and even sneakers.

A LOOK AT HOW FOSSIL FUELS ARE USED (BY RANK)

FOSSIL FUEL	MAJOR PRODUCERS	USE OF FOSSIL FUEL
Oil	Saudi Arabia, Russia, U.S.	• As gasoline, diesel fuel, jet fuel to power cars, buses, trains, and planes • Heating oil • In the manufacturing of plastics, nylon, polyester, cosmetics, medicines, fertilizers, and insecticides
Coal	China, U.S., India	• Fuel for heat, light, and generating electricity
Natural Gas	U.S., Russia, Canada	• Fuel for light, heat, cooking, manufacturing, and generating electricity

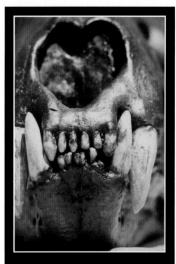

LA BREA: TREASURE TROVE OF DEATH

Tar pits form when **crude oil** (raw, untreated petroleum) from Earth's crust seeps up through cracks to the surface. The La Brea Tar Pits in California contained animal and plant **fossils** from 1.8 million to 10,000 years ago. The pits held the remains of insects, reptiles, amphibians, birds, fish, and even mammals, such as saber-toothed tigers (above).

OIL IN DEMAND

Uses for oil continue to increase. Quantities of it, however, continue to decrease.

Many nations have large supplies of oil beneath their land. One-third of the largest oil-supplying nations are in the Middle East. The five nations that use the most oil are the United States, Japan, China, Germany, and Russia. The demand for oil often affects the relationships between countries that have oil and countries that need it.

This container ship is powered by diesel, an oil-based fuel. Much of its cargo consists of oil-based products. The containers that hold the cargo are made of oil-based materials. And the hold of this ship is probably carrying oil, which will power other means of transportation.

In large urban settings such as Los Angeles (right), the burning of fossil fuels releases pollutants into the air. Exhaust from cars, trucks, and other vehicles are major causes.

PROBLEMS WITH FOSSIL FUEL RESERVES

Humans have come up with many uses for coal, natural gas, and oil. Use of those fossil fuels causes some problems, however. Most fossil fuels must be burned to release their energy. Only then do they create heat, produce electricity, or otherwise perform as we need them to. As they burn, however, they release **pollutants**, or substances that are harmful to the environment.

Pollutants include certain gases that cause urban **smog**, air pollution, **acid rain**, and **global warming**. Acid rain occurs when air pollution mixes with water in the **atmosphere**. The atmosphere is the layer of air that surrounds Earth. Global warming is a gradual warming of Earth's atmosphere.

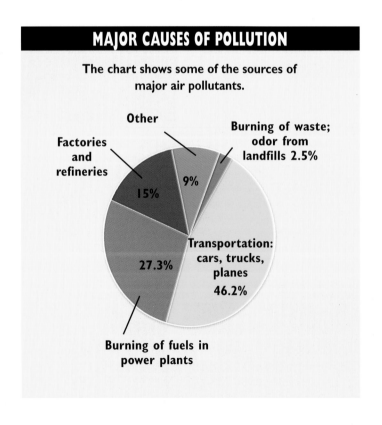

MAJOR CAUSES OF POLLUTION

The chart shows some of the sources of major air pollutants.

Other

Factories and refineries
15%

9%

Burning of waste; odor from landfills 2.5%

Transportation: cars, trucks, planes
46.2%

27.3%

Burning of fuels in power plants

In strip mining (above), surface soil is stripped away to get at the coal beneath. Strip mining destroys plant life and can result in soil erosion.

A RISKY BUSINESS

Aside from the pollution, getting to these fossil fuels is difficult. They are often buried deep underground, where they formed. They are brought to the surface by mining, drilling, piping, or other means. Those methods can be harmful to people and to the planet.

OIL SPILLS

Oil spills are a danger whenever crude oil is transported. Spills can kill animals and pollute water. They can also harm communities and industries along the coasts. In 1979, the tanker *Atlantic Empress* collided with the tanker *Aegean Captain*. The two ships spilled 304,237 tons (276,000 metric tons) of oil into the Caribbean Sea. It was one of the worst oil tanker spills on record.

MINERALS AND ROCK RESOURCES

Minerals and rocks are nonrenewable resources. They make up Earth's crust and other solid parts of our planet.

A HUGE AND VARIED RESOURCE

Scientists have identified more than 3,000 different minerals. Some, such as ores, contain metals. The metals can be removed for use in building and in manufacturing. They are especially useful in electrical supplies. Metal is a good conductor of heat and electricity. Rare minerals, such as rubies and emeralds, are used in jewelry. So are precious metals, such as gold and silver.

NOT JUST YOUR MOTHER'S JEWELRY

Many diamonds come from Africa. Russia, Canada, Australia, and Brazil are also big diamond suppliers. Once mined, diamonds have many uses. They are cut and polished to become expensive jewelry. As the hardest mineral known, diamonds are also used for cutting, polishing, and grinding.

A specific mineral always has the same makeup. That gives it a very identifiable look. This mineral is quartz.

Like any other mineral, salt must be taken from the earth. Here, workers gather the mineral from the Colchani Salt Pans in Bolivia. The salt pans are large plains made entirely of salt.

METALS: A USEFUL RESOURCE

Metals are often removed from other resources, such as minerals. A metal can be combined with other substances. That mix of materials is called an **alloy**.

NICKEL
Nickel is used mostly as an alloy. Combined with iron, it gives great strength to steel. The nickel used in coins is actually an alloy made up mostly of copper.

TUNGSTEN
Tungsten is the most heat-resistant metal. It melts at 6,170° Fahrenheit (3,410° Celsius). It is used as the filament in light bulbs.

ALUMINUM
Aluminum is lightweight yet strong. It can be shaped easily when heated and stays tough in extreme cold. Aluminum is one of the most useful metals. It is used for foil, cans, and in building materials.

A STABLE AND RELIABLE RESOURCE

The term *mineral* refers to specific substances. A true mineral has a certain chemical makeup. It has the same makeup no matter where it is found. This is not true of rocks. Samples of the same type of rock may have very different chemical makeups.

PROPERTIES OF MINERALS: A GEMSTONE GLOSSARY

Color: A mineral's color affects its beauty and value. Some minerals always have the same color, such as gold. Others come in different colors. For example, topaz can be yellow, pink, red, or blue.

Hardness: The Mohs scale measures the hardness of minerals. The scale ranges from 1 (softest) to 10 (hardest). Diamond, the hardest mineral, is rated 10. Quartz is rated 7.

Luster: Luster is the way a mineral's surface reflects light. It describes how brilliant or dull a mineral looks. Some minerals appear glossy. Others look pearly, silky, or waxy.

Transparency: Transparency is a measure of light that passes through a mineral. Some minerals are highly transparent. They let most light pass through them. Others are opaque (oh-PAYK), letting no light through.

COPPER

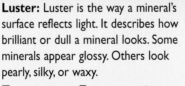

MICA

AMETHYST

CHAPTER 3:
Renewable Resources

Earth's renewable resources can be replaced in a short amount of time. Energy from the Sun, water, wind, and animals and plants are all renewable resources.

SMART AND NECESSARY

The air we breathe and heat produced inside Earth are resources. Water, sunlight, and plants are crucial to life on the planet. Taking care of Earth's renewable resources isn't just smart. It is necessary.

RENEWABLE RESOURCES AT WORK

An **ecosystem** is a community in nature. It is any place where plants and animals depend on each other for food. Within that ecosystem, the animals and plants are a renewable resource. The animals and plants also depend on other renewable resources, such as water and the Sun.

Plants rely on the soil and the atmosphere for water and carbon dioxide. They use energy from sunlight to convert the carbon dioxide and water into food.

Water. Air. Wind. Sun. A number of renewable resources are available to us every day. Earth has more renewable than nonrenewable resources.

Honeybees, birds, and other animals eat plants or drink their nectar. In turn, those animals help carry out **pollination**. They carry pollen from one plant to another. That helps the plants reproduce.

Meat-eating animals eat plant-eating animals. The plant **nutrients** then enter the meat eaters' bodies.

When plants, insects, and other organisms die, their decaying remains add nutrients to the soil. That provides nourishment to worms and insects.

HELPING ECOSYSTEMS HELP THEMSELVES

Adding or removing a renewable resource can alter an ecosystem. By monitoring Earth's ecosystems, we can help nature maintain a healthy balance of plants and animals.

CUTTING DOWN WITH CARE
Forests can stay renewable as long as people help forests replace lost trees. Controlled logging keeps forests free of sick or dying trees.

MANAGING ANIMAL NUMBERS
Controlling animal **populations** assures food for all. Fish won't have enough to eat if there are too many of them in one place. **Overfishing**, however, can upset the balance of plant and animal life.

WATER FOR ALL
Dams control the flow of water and create lakes and **reservoirs**. These provide a source of drinking water and **habitats** for wildlife.

THE WATER CYCLE

*The Sun drives the **water cycle** that moves water around our Earth.*

*2. The warm gas rises in the air, where it cools and forms tiny droplets. That is called **condensation**.*

*3. As the drops get heavier, they fall as rain or snow. That is called **precipitation**.*

*1. The Sun warms the sea's surface, causing the water to turn into vapor. That is called **evaporation**.*

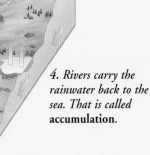

*4. Rivers carry the rainwater back to the sea. That is called **accumulation**.*

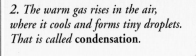

ALTERNATIVE ENERGY SOURCES

Today, only a fraction of the energy we use comes from renewable resources. In the future, however, that could change. Other energy sources offer some exciting possibilities. Some renewable energy sources, such as **solar power**, **wind power**, and hydroelectric power, are already in use. Others are being tested or are not yet widely used.

Heated water from this geothermal power plant in Iceland flows to a famous health spa called Blue Lagoon.

GEOTHERMAL POWER

Geothermal power comes from using the heat of the Earth itself. This heat, in the form of hot water and steam, is often found in areas of volcanic activity. With pipes and pumps, the water or steam is taken from underground reservoirs. It is then used to power turbines. A turbine is a device with a part that rotates to produce electricity.

TIDAL POWER

Like hydroelectric power, **tidal power** also uses energy from water. The energy is generated by changing tides in oceans and large lakes. Dams stretching over bays capture water at high tide. Later, the water is released with the outgoing tide. The movement of water powers turbines and generates electricity.

WIND POWER

Wind power is created by capturing the power of wind. In the past, people used windmills. Today, they use powerful wind turbines. Both get energy from wind, using it to turn blades at the top of a tower. A modern wind turbine's turning blades are used to produce electricity.

Wind power is renewable, and it doesn't pollute. But some people don't like a landscape dotted with giant wind turbines, as seen here in California.

ALTERNATIVE ENERGIES AT WORK

SOLAR POWER

Solar power comes from the Sun. Energy from the Sun is collected by capturing its rays in special solar panels. That energy is converted to electricity. Some buildings use solar panels for heating and cooling. The parking meter shown above is powered by a solar panel.

HYDROELECTRIC POWER

Moving water generates hydroelectric power. Power plants built over flowing rivers convert the water's energy into electricity. First the water is stored behind a dam. As the water is released, the movement turns huge turbine blades. That, in turn, generates electricity.

SOLAR-POWERED SUN TEA

ⓘ The Sun's energy is there for the taking. Test that idea by making yourself some Sun tea. Even on a slightly gray day, you can use the Sun's energy to heat water and brew a container of tea.

Materials needed
- a large clear jug or container (with cover)
- cold water
- 2–6 tea bags, depending on the size of the container
- glasses, lots of ice, lemon, and sugar or an artificial sweetener

1) Fill your container with water. Add the tea bags. Place the container in a sunny place. Allow the tea to brew in the sunlight for several hours.

2) When the tea is a dark color, remove the tea bags. Refrigerate your Sun tea or add plenty of ice to cool it. You can flavor the drink with lemon and sugar or sweetener. Then enjoy your solar-powered tea!

THE OXYGEN CYCLE

Plants take in carbon dioxide and water. They use sunlight to change these substances into food and oxygen. That is called **photosynthesis.**

Plants absorb carbon dioxide and give off oxygen.

Animals and people breathe in the oxygen and breathe out carbon dioxide.

PLANT RESOURCES

It would be easy to overlook plants as valuable natural resources. They are so much a part of our lives. As part of the oxygen cycle, plants play a key role in renewing the oxygen in Earth's atmosphere. Without plants, humans and animals would not have oxygen to breathe.

Plants are also a food resource in all of Earth's ecosystems. Humans eat plants that grow wild. People also grow crops as food.

RAIN FOREST TREASURE

Many scientists think that about two-thirds of the world's plant species grow in rain forests. These plants produce as much as 40 percent of Earth's oxygen. Rain forest plants give us hundreds of different fruits, vegetables, spices, and other foods. The raw materials for many products, from chewing gum to rubber, come from rain forest trees.

MEDICINE CABINET TO THE WORLD

Scientists estimate that about 25 percent of the world's medicines are based on ingredients found in rain forest plants. Some plants contain compounds that help heal wounds. Others are made into drugs that fight cancer. Scientists study rain forest plants in search of new medicines.

Warm, wet rain forests (like this one in Madagascar, in Africa) have more kinds of trees than anywhere else on Earth. Protecting rain forests helps protect countless kinds of plants and animals.

BIOMES — MAPPING EARTH'S NATURAL RESOURCES

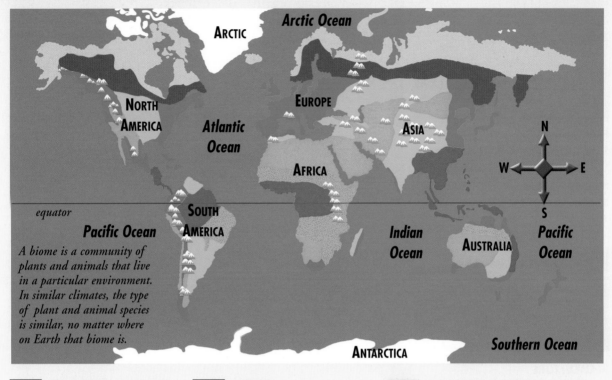

ARCTIC

Arctic Ocean

NORTH AMERICA

Atlantic Ocean

EUROPE

ASIA

AFRICA

N
W — E
S

equator

Pacific Ocean

SOUTH AMERICA

Indian Ocean

AUSTRALIA

Pacific Ocean

A biome is a community of plants and animals that live in a particular environment. In similar climates, the type of plant and animal species is similar, no matter where on Earth that biome is.

Southern Ocean

ANTARCTICA

TEMPERATE GRASSLANDS
Warm, dry summers, cool or cold winters; rainfall supports lots of plant and animal life

TUNDRA
Cold, windy plains; soil freezes just below surface; plants need short roots to absorb nutrients

TEMPERATE DECIDUOUS FOREST
Shrubby coastal area; plants and animals adapted to hot, dry summers and mild winters

SAVANNA
Large plains with scattered trees and bushes; amount of plant life determined by amount of rainfall

ARCTIC/ANTARCTICA
Extremely cold and dry all year; frozen ground and icy seas; little plant life

CONIFEROUS FOREST
Cold evergreen forest; most animals migrate or hibernate in winter

DESERT
Dry land, little rain; plant life includes cacti, which store water

OCEAN
Saltwater environment supports a huge variety of marine life

TROPICAL RAIN FOREST
Hot, wet climate that supports a huge variety of life

PAPER OR FORESTS?

It's no secret that Earth's rain forests are in danger. About 78 million acres of rain forest are cut down every year to create farmland and to supply wood and paper products. About 95 percent of all paper is made from wood. But paper can be recycled and reused. Think of how much rain forest could be saved just by recycling the daily newspaper!*

* See the newspaper recycling experiment on page 29.

ANIMALS AT WORK

PACK ANIMALS

Some animals have many uses. Llamas, like camels, horses, and even elephants, are called pack animals. That means they are used to carry things. Llamas also have wool that can be made into yarn.

AQUACULTURE

Some fish, such as salmon and trout, are both caught in the wild and farmed. Fish farming is known as aquaculture. As wild fish supplies have declined, fish farming has grown. Today, about 43 percent of all food fish come from farms.

WHOSE RESOURCE?

The North American northern spotted owl prefers nesting in old-growth forests. The owl became the focus of a debate between **conservationists** and logging companies. The conservationists wanted to protect the owl's habitat. The loggers wanted to harvest the valuable wood.

ANIMAL RESOURCES

Just like plants, animals are a renewable resource. For people, animals are sources of food and other products. Sheep, goats, and cattle provide milk and meat. Hides from many animals are used for clothing and shoes.

Animals also have a major effect on the environment. For example, some ranchers complain that coyotes kill their sheep. But coyotes also control the rodent population around farms. Each animal plays an important role in keeping its own ecosystem balanced.

Some animals, such as cattle, are such important resources that humans have domesticated, or tamed, them. People all over the world keep herds of cattle.

THE BIG PICTURE

Our planet is a collection of ecosystems. Each individual ecosystem contributes to the overall health of our planet. Sometimes, however, humans upset the balance of an ecosystem. We cut down too many trees in a rain forest, for instance, or damage the landscape when mining for coal. We have to think about how our actions affect the planet as a whole.

GO WILD WHERE YOU LIVE!

Exploring the wildlife where you live gives you a chance to see nature up close. That may lead to some surprise discoveries! Try the following activities to learn more about the natural resources near your home.

1) Use online or library sources to find out what kinds of wildlife live in your area. You can also visit a local zoo or nature center.

2) Observe life around you! Track birds, insects, and other animals you see near your home. Write your observations in a notebook for one week.

3) Pay attention to the resources in your area. What do the animals you see rely on to survive? Are the resources organic or inorganic? Are they natural or made by humans?

4) Identify some ways in which the animals' resources might be threatened. For example, are homes, stores, factories, or offices being built in underdeveloped areas? Is a river in your area becoming polluted by trash?

THE AMERICAN BISON

In the 1800s, bison populations on the Great Plains may have been as great as 75 million. Native Americans used the bison for food and to make clothing, shelters, and tools. Non-Native settlers hunted the bison aggressively until it was almost extinct. By the 1880s, the bison population may have been as low as 1,000. The government and conservationists worked to protect the bison, and the population grew. But bison will never reach the huge numbers of the past.

WATER USE IN THE HOME

Here are some common uses of water in the home. Also shown is the average amount of water each activity uses.

- One bath: 21 gallons (80 liters)

- One shower: 9.2 gallons (35 liters)

- One toilet flush: 2 gallons (8 liters)

- One dishwasher load: 6.6 gallons (25 liters)

- One washing machine load: 17.2 gallons (65 liters)

In an average home, which activity do you think uses the most water per day?

[Answer: flushing the toilet]

CHAPTER 4:
What Can You Do?

Taking care of our natural resources will help ensure that people have what they need to survive in the future. Are you responsible caretakers of the world?

REDUCE

You may have heard the expression "Reduce, reuse, recycle." That slogan reminds people of three things we can all do to cut down on our use of natural resources.

We need to protect our natural resources for generations to come.

Cutting down on the amount of oil we use can help conserve fossil fuels. That's important, because fossil fuels are a nonrenewable resource. Burning less oil would also reduce air pollution. Many cities are working toward providing "clean" mass transit. In the future, you might ride on buses and trains powered by electricity, solar power, or other renewable forms of energy.

Sometimes, reducing our energy use can improve our health. Riding a bike or walking instead of driving benefits both the planet and you!

HOW MUCH DO YOU USE?

How much water do you use? Try this experiment to figure out how much water you might use in one year by just washing your hands.

Materials needed
- large bowl
- a large measuring cup

1) Place a large bowl in your sink to catch the water you use as you wash your hands. Pour the used water into a measuring cup. How much did you use? Record the amount in a notebook.

2) Keep track of how many times you wash your hands in a day. Multiply that number by the amount of water you recorded earlier. The result tells you how much water you use, on average, in a day.

3) Multiply the amount of water you use in one day by 365. That result tells you how much water you use each year just by washing your hands. Did the total surprise you?

TAKING IT EASY WITH ENERGY

PLANNING FOR THE FUTURE
Some energy-saving solutions are costly to put in place. It costs more to install solar panels on a home than it does to put in an oil or gas heating system. Over time, however, solar panels save homeowners' money. Energy from the Sun is free, while oil is expensive. Solar panels also reduce our need for fossil fuels.

EVERY LITTLE BIT COUNTS
Your local electricity or water company has tips on saving energy. Your family can get showerheads and toilets that use less water. You can turn down the heat by a few degrees in winter and wear a sweater!

EARTHWORM COMPOSTERS

Did you know that potato peels, apple cores, and eggshells can all be recycled? Over time, worms and bacteria break down that organic matter and turn it into very rich soil called compost.

Some people use earthworm boxes to make compost. The plastic or wooden boxes are filled with shredded newspaper or cardboard and decaying leaves. A handful of dirt is also added to the mix. Dirt is gritty and helps worms break down food particles. Boxes can be made at home or bought from garden supply stores.

In the box, earthworms eat kitchen scraps such as fruit and vegetable peels, bread, and eggshells. (Do not add meat scraps.) Each earthworm can eat its own weight in waste every 24 hours. The worms' droppings mix with the dirt in the box to make nutrient-filled compost. In this way, organic waste is recycled to create a garden fertilizer!

REUSE

In addition to reducing our need for resources, reusing and recycling help conserve natural resources. Reusing allows us to make a second (or third or fourth) use of an existing object. Think about the shopping bag you carried into the kitchen. Could you use it again? Many items can be used more than once.

RECYCLE

Recycling allows us to make new things out of used materials. Many materials can be recycled, such as paper, plastic, metal, and glass. Many of these materials are already part of recycling programs.

Most communities have recycling programs that allow us all to easily dispose of metal cans, soda bottles, and newspapers. Such programs give us a chance to help conserve our planet's natural resources.

This paper was collected from recycling bins. It will soon be processed and recycled.

Recycling bottles, cans, and paper is one of the easiest ways to save natural resources.

MAKE RECYCLED PAPER

ⓘ The newspapers and scrap paper you take to the recycling center are turned into pulp. The pulp is then turned back into paper. Follow these instructions to make your own recycled paper!

Materials needed
- a cookie sheet
- a mixing bowl
- 3 cups of water
- a newspaper
- a rolling pin

1) Tear one or two pages of newspaper into small pieces of 1 inch (2.5 cm) or less.

2) Put some of the paper pieces into a large bowl. Add all the water. Add the remaining paper. Tear and squeeze the paper until you get a mush that looks like thick oatmeal.

3) Using your fingers, spread about 1 cup of the paper pulp over an upside-down cookie sheet. Be sure to spread the pulp evenly.

4) Lay several full sheets of newspaper over the pulp. Carefully turn the cookie sheet over. When you remove the cookie sheet, your pulp layer should be sitting on the newspaper.

5) Fold the edges of the newspaper to cover the pulp. Roll the rolling pin over the newspaper package to squeeze out extra water.

6) Uncover the pulp and let it dry completely. You have just made a sheet of recycled paper!

GLOSSARY

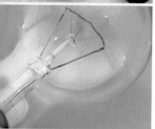

accumulation: the process of something building up or collecting. In the water cycle, accumulation is the stage in which water remains for a period of time underground, in the ocean, or in another body of water.

acid rain: air pollution mixed with water in the atmosphere that then falls to Earth as rain

alloy: a substance made by combining metal with another material

atmosphere: the thick layer of air that surrounds Earth

condensation: the process in which a gas changes to a liquid

conservation: the planned management of natural resources

conservationist: a person who works to protect Earth's natural resources

crude oil: the natural state of petroleum. This fossil fuel is formed from decaying plants, animals, and other organisms.

crust: the outer layer of Earth that consists of landforms and the ocean floor. The crust is about 25 miles (40 km) at its thickest point.

ecosystem: a community in which animals and plants rely on each other and on resources such as water and sunlight. An ecosystem can be large, like a woodland, or small, like a single tree.

erosion: the wearing away of material by water, wind, or glacial ice

evaporation: the process in which a liquid changes to a gas, such as when liquid water turns to water vapor

extinct: having completely died out

fossil: remains or imprint of an ancient plant or animal that has been preserved in rocks

fossil fuels: fuels that began as the decaying remains of animals, plants, and other organisms. They include oil, natural gas, and coal.

freshwater: water sources, such as most rivers and lakes, that do not contain salt

gemstone: a precious rocks or mineral, such as a ruby, emerald, or pearl, that is often used in jewelry

geothermal power: energy, such as electricity, that is created by harnessing heat from within Earth

glacier: a large body of ice moving slowly down a slope or over a wide area of land

global warming: the gradual warming of the Earth's atmosphere. Most scientists believe that this is partly caused by humans burning fossils fuels, such as oil and coal.

habitat: an environment in which a particular plant or animal does best and is most likely found

hydroelectric power: electricity produced by power plants that use the energy created by moving water

inorganic: something that is not living, such as metal or rock

irrigation: the process of bringing water to a place; for example, pumping water from a river to irrigate (water) crops

mineral: solid, usually inorganic, substance that occurs naturally on Earth, such as gold, copper, or salt

natural resources: the materials, energy sources, and living things found in nature that are useful to people and other living creatures

nonrenewable resource: a resource that cannot be renewed, or replaced. Fossil fuels and minerals are nonrenewable.

nuclear energy: energy stored in the nucleus, or core, of the atom that is released and used to make electricity

nutrients: a mineral or another substance that plants and animals need to grow and develop

ores: minerals that contain valuable materials such as metal. Ores are mined for the materials that they contain.

organic: something that is living, such as an animal or plant

organism: a living being

overfishing: catching so many of a specific type of fish population that the fish does not have time to breed, which causes its population to drop

petroleum: the substance, created by decaying plant and animal remains, from which oil, gas, and other products come

photosynthesis: the process by which green plants form carbohydrates from carbon dioxide and water in the presence of light

pollinate: to transfer pollen from one plant to another, in preparation for plant reproduction

pollutant: anything that makes a substance dirty or impure

population: the people or things living in a certain place

precipitation: any form of water, such as rain or snow, that falls to Earth's surface

renewable resource: a resource that can be renewed, or replaced. Plants and animals are renewable resources.

reservoir: a place where water is stored for future use

salt water: water, such as ocean water, that contains dissolved salts

sediments: tiny grains of materials, such as soil and sand

smog: a foglike haze caused by pollution in the air. The word is formed by combining the words *smoke* and *fog*.

solar power: power created by harnessing the energy of the Sun as it reaches Earth

tidal power: energy produced by the natural rise and fall in bodies of water in oceans and lakes

water cycle: the constant movement of water from the air to land and back to the air

wind power: capturing the energy of the wind, which can be used to drive turbines and produce electrical energy